FANTASTIC FAILS

Learning from Bad Ideas

MEDICAL MISHAPS

BY ELIZABETH PAGEL-HOGAN

CAPSTONE PRESS
a capstone imprint

Capstone Captivate is published by Capstone Press,
an imprint of Capstone.
1710 Roe Crest Drive
North Mankato, Minnesota 56003
www.capstonepub.com

Copyright © 2020 by Capstone. All rights reserved.
No part of this publication may be reproduced in whole or in part, or stored in a retrieval system, or transmitted in any form or by any means, electronic, mechanical, photocopying, recording, or otherwise, without written permission of the publisher.

Library of Congress Cataloging-in-Publication Data is available on the Library of Congress website.
ISBN: 978-1-5435-9213-9 (library binding)
ISBN: 978-1-4966-6622-2 (paperback)
ISBN: 978-1-5435-9217-7 (eBook PDF)

Summary: See some of the world's most messed-up medical mishaps at a microscopic level. Find out how each procedure, tool, or surgery failed, the basic science that was missed, and what doctors learned from their mistakes.

Image Credits
Alamy: Charles Walker Collection, 5, Science History Images, 9, 18, 26; Getty Images: Bettmann, 34, Stringer/Kurt Hutton, 42; Library of Congress: 25; Newscom: akg-images, 6, Heritage Images/CM Dixon, 22, Heritage Images/The Print Collector, 21; Science Source: Health Protection Agency, 37, Wellcome Images, 41; Shutterstock: Andrew Mayovskyy, 44 (bottom), blambca, cover, Chaiyawat Chaidet, 45 (bottom), Kallayanee Naloka, 30, Lane V. Erickson, 44 (top), Monkey Business Images, 45 (top), Sergei Primakov, 14, sfam_photo, cover (background), Sirirat, 10; SuperStock: Bridgeman Art Library, London, 13, Iberfoto, 29, Pantheon, 17; Wikimedia: Public Domain, 33, Sam LaRussa, 38

Design Elements: Shutterstock

Editorial Credits
Editor: Mari Bolte; Designer: Jennifer Bergstrom; Media Researcher: Eric Gohl; Production Specialist: Laura Manthe

All internet sites appearing in back matter were available and accurate when this book was sent to press.

Printed and bound in the United States of America.
PA100

TABLE OF CONTENTS

CHAPTER

1 NOT FUNNY!
THE FOUR HUMORS 4

2 WHAT'S THAT SMELL?
URINALYSIS 8

3 BLOODY BUSINESS
BLOODLETTING 12

4 SHARING ISN'T CARING
BLOOD TRANSFUSIONS 16

5 A REAL HEADACHE!
TREPANNING 20

6 ATTACKING FROM THE INSIDE OUT
GERM THEORY TO VACCINATIONS 24

7 MOLDY MEDICINE
PENICILLIN 28

8 SHOCKING SICKNESS
ELECTRIC THERAPY 32

9 JUST ZAP IT
RADIATION THERAPY 36

10 MY HEAD HURTS!
LOBOTOMIES 40

MEDICINE MOVES ALONG 44
GLOSSARY 46
READ MORE 47
INTERNET SITES 47
INDEX 48

Words in **bold** are in the glossary.

THROUGHOUT HUMAN HISTORY, people have gotten sick or injured. Medical workers and healers have been around equally as long. Unfortunately, their ideas of what was wrong with their patients—and how to heal them—weren't always right. Find out more about the mistakes that were made, and how doctors fixed them.

CHAPTER 1
NOT FUNNY!
THE FOUR HUMORS

Hippocrates (circa 460–380 BC) was a doctor in ancient Greece. He taught his students to watch their patients and write down their **symptoms**. Today, doctors take an oath based off Hippocrates's teachings. They pledge to take their patients' best interests into account and to act ethically.

Early Greek physicians like Hippocrates thought that the human body was made up of four humors. The four humors were blood, phlegm, yellow bile, and black bile. Each humor was connected to a part of the human body.

It was also connected to a natural force, and a season. Each humor was either hot or cold and either wet or dry. When a person was sick, it was thought that the humors were out of balance.

the four humors

The Doctor Will See You Now

Some historians believe the first known doctor was an Egyptian called Imhotep. Imhotep lived in the 2600s BC. He made medicines from plants. The first known hospitals were created in India in 226 BC by a ruler named Ashoka.

When a Greek doctor thought a person's humors were out of balance, he or she tried to fix it. A fever was thought to mean too much yellow bile. That signified fire, sun, and heat. So the patient was ordered to take a cold bath. This was generally harmless.

Hippocrates became known as the Father of Medicine and the Great Physician.

But if the doctors thought a patient had too much phlegm or black bile, they might give hellebore. Hellebore is a poisonous plant. It made people sneeze, throw up, and have diarrhea. It was thought that this would help the patient get rid of the extra phlegm or black bile. But hellebore really made people very sick. Sometimes they died.

FACT: Ancient Chinese physicians believed good health was a balance between two life forces, yin and yang.

Lessons Learned

Doctors now know that sickness isn't caused by a problem with four humors. Even though Greek doctors had some great ideas for medicine, they also made big mistakes.

CHAPTER 2
WHAT'S THAT SMELL?

URINALYSIS

Checking a sick person's urine, called urinalysis or uroscopy, is a way to **diagnose** illness. It is a useful tool to check for infections, diabetes, pregnancy, and other changes in the body. Though the idea of using urine as a way to tell if someone is sick is a good one, the ideas about why someone was sick weren't always right.

In historical times, doctors would note the smell, quantity, and **concentration** of the urine. They looked for things floating in the urine. They used a color wheel to compare shades. They even tasted it. This seems gross, but it was useful. If the urine tasted sweet, doctors knew the person had what modern doctors know as diabetes.

FACT: Manipal Hospital in India holds the world record for most urinalysis tests performed in a day. On March 13, 2019, medical staff performed 623 tests over eight hours. The event raised awareness for kidney health.

Urinalysis reagent strips can help doctors get a quick and accurate view of a patient's health.

Checking urine was a good place to start. But some early doctors had incorrect ideas about how certain signs were related to health.

One doctor suggested that bubbles at the top of the urine sample meant a person was sick in his or her head. But if doctors saw materials sinking to the bottom of the urine sample, a person's sickness was in the lower part of the body. Some people even claimed to tell a person's fortune from his or her urine.

Doctors started to think they could figure out everything wrong with a sick person just from urine. They stopped examining patients thoroughly. In response, patients started testing their doctors by bringing them other people's urine. For some time, people stopped trusting urinalysis.

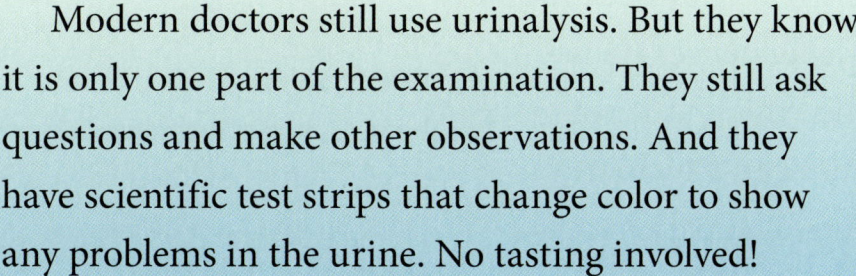

Lessons Learned

Modern doctors still use urinalysis. But they know it is only one part of the examination. They still ask questions and make other observations. And they have scientific test strips that change color to show any problems in the urine. No tasting involved!

CHAPTER 3
Bloody Business

BLOODLETTING

Bloodletting has been used around the world for more than 3,000 years. The ancient Egyptians were the first recorded people to do it. Sometimes it helped. But it could also kill.

Throughout history, blades called thumb lancets or fleams have been used to cut a person's vein. The blood from the vein would be caught in a bowl. A patient would be bled until the doctor felt enough of the "bad" blood had been removed.

Benjamin Rush (1746–1813) was a respected doctor and teacher. He wrote America's first chemistry textbook. He signed the Declaration of Independence. He is called the "Father of American **Psychiatry**." He treated patients during **yellow fever**

FACT: Yellow fever is carried by mosquitos. It starts with fevers, chills, and body pains. Later it can cause bleeding, **shock**, and organ failure.

outbreaks in the North American colonies. But he also believed the fever was caused by bad blood. Some of his patients had 80 percent of their blood removed as a result.

Some doctors believed that blood was the most important humor.

Losing a little blood doesn't hurt people very much. The average human body has about 1.3 gallons (5 liters) of blood. When you donate blood, you give about 1 pint (0.5 L) at a time. This is something healthy people usually have no problem doing.

MEDICINAL LEECHES

Leeches are a safe method of bloodletting. They suck a small amount of blood from animals they bite. Using leeches can reduce swelling and increase blood flow in injuries.

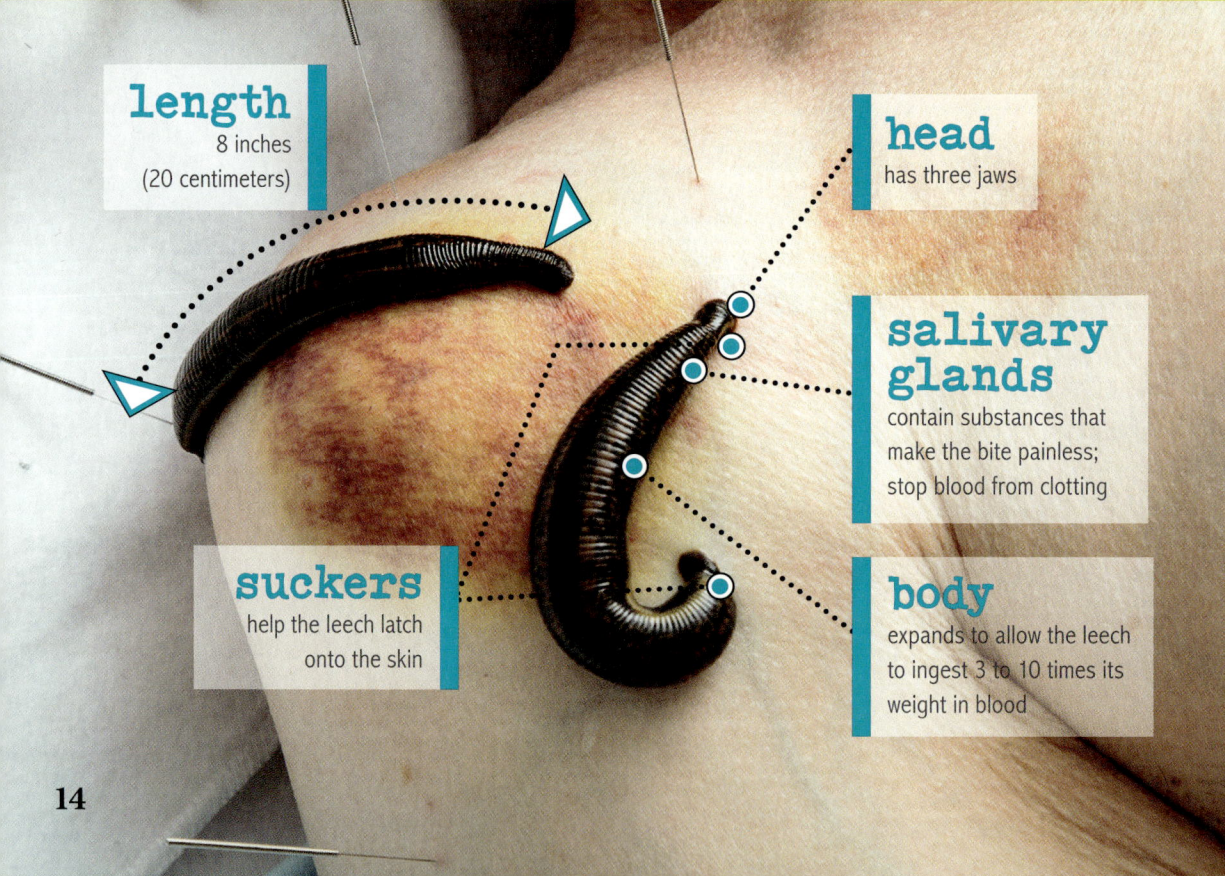

length
8 inches (20 centimeters)

head
has three jaws

salivary glands
contain substances that make the bite painless; stop blood from clotting

suckers
help the leech latch onto the skin

body
expands to allow the leech to ingest 3 to 10 times its weight in blood

But sometimes doctors removed too much blood. Losing too much blood can cause a dangerous drop in blood pressure. It can also cause a heart attack or send the patient into shock. Blood keeps your organs working. Without enough blood, they can fail. Instead of getting better, some bloodletting patients died.

Rush was sued by a journalist who accused him of killing patients. Rush won the case. But by then his practice of overbleeding patients had turned many doctors against him.

Lessons Learned

By the end of the 1800s, people knew that bloodletting wasn't a cure-all. Doctors learned that patients needed most of their blood. But the practice of bloodletting still exists today. Sometimes it can help with certain blood diseases or infections. Leeches are also sometimes used in modern medicine today.

CHAPTER 4
SHARING ISN'T CARING

BLOOD TRANSFUSIONS

Physicians knew blood was important to the human body. But, as bloodletting shows, they didn't always have the right ideas about this important fluid.

The first recorded **blood transfusion** was done in the mid-1660s. Dr. Richard Lower took blood from a healthy dog. He gave that blood to an injured dog. The injured dog lived. But Lower took too much blood from the healthy dog, and it died.

Lower proved that the idea worked. But he, and other doctors, still didn't understand blood. They believed blood controlled a person's personality and behavior. One thought a blood transfusion could help a man who was aggressive and

FACT: Human and animal blood are usually not compatible. The first humans who received transfusions of animal blood lived, but only because such a small amount of animal blood was added to their own.

angry. He replaced the "angry" blood with the blood of a pure and innocent animal—a calf or a lamb. But the new blood didn't change the man's behavior.

Since the man's personality stayed the same, most people thought blood transfusions were a trick. Others believed that blood transfusions could be used to create monsters.

Blood transfusions from animals to humans was made illegal in the mid-1670s.

Some people still died after blood transfusions. Sadly, doctors and physicians didn't know viruses could be transmitted through blood. People receiving blood transfusions were sometimes infected with viruses before scientists learned how to check blood and make sure it was safe. In 1900, blood types were discovered, which made safe blood transfusions even easier.

In 1914, a way to keep blood from clotting was discovered. Before this, blood transfusions needed to be done with the patient and donor together.

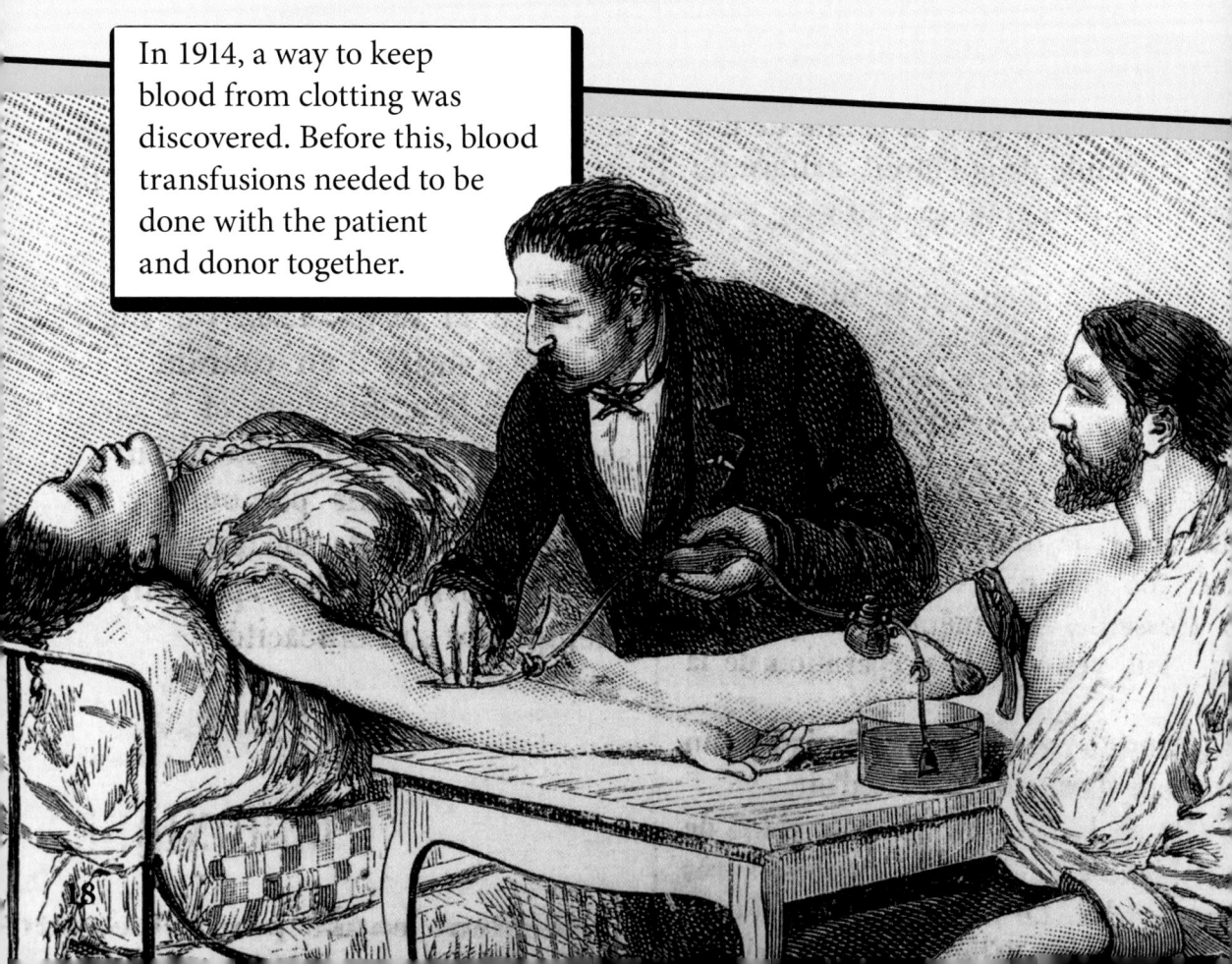

Lessons Learned

Dr. Bernard Fantus opened the first blood bank in 1937. His research meant that blood could be preserved, stored, and transported for later use. More than 4.5 million people are saved every year through blood transfusion. Although the first transfusions had mixed results, what doctors were able to learn has saved millions of lives since.

Blood Types

There are four major blood groups—A, B, O, and AB. There are also proteins called the Rh factor. If a blood has the protein, a + is shown. If it is absent, it is marked with a –. The eight most common blood types are A+, A-, B+, B-, O+, O-, AB+, and AB-. For safe and successful transfusions, the blood types between the donor and the patient must match (A+ to A+, B- to B-). People with O- blood are known as universal donors. They can give blood to anyone.

Chapter 5
A Real Headache!
Trepanning

One of the oldest forms of surgery is trepanning, or trepanation. Drilling, cutting, or scraping holes in human skulls was done as far back as prehistoric times and around the world. In 2016, an archaeologist claimed to have found a 7,000-year-old skull with a trepanation hole.

Headaches were a common reason for trepanning. Doctors thought headaches happened when a person had a "badness" in his or her head.

Sometimes they drilled holes if a person acted in strange and unusual ways. They blamed evil spirits for the person's behavior. They believed the hole would let the evil spirits out of the person's head. In some cultures, people kept the piece of bone that was removed from their skulls

FACT: The word *trepan* comes from a Greek word for "a borer." Borers are tools used to make holes.

and wore it to protect them from other bad spirits. In ancient Egypt, potions were made out of the skull pieces.

Drills, scraping tools, and other objects used for trepanation have been found by archaeologists.

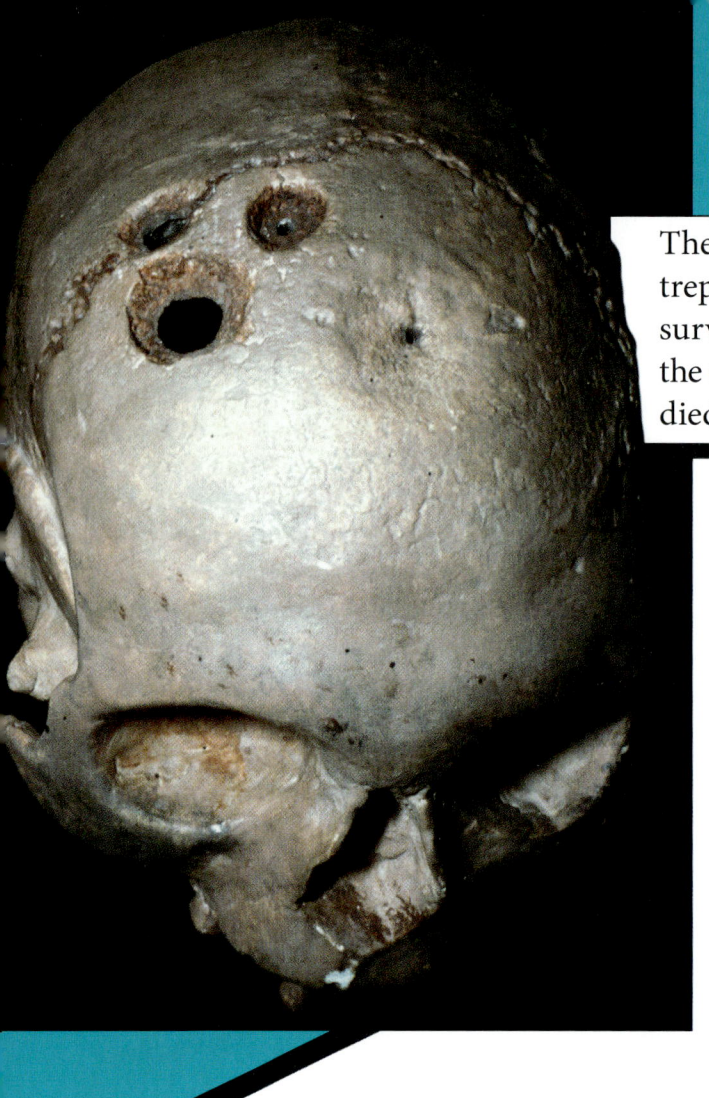

The owner of this skull had three trepanations performed. He survived the first operation, but the others were less successful. He died after the third procedure.

Trepanning was also done when someone suffered a head injury. Someone hit in the head with a club might have swelling from blood collecting under his or her skull. In this case, drilling a hole would help let out the blood and relieve the swelling.

Sometimes the person did not live through the surgery. Others lived only a few weeks or months afterward. They would be exposed to infection through the hole in their heads. The practice also exposed the dura mater, the protective **membrane** around the brain. And sometimes the surgery would have to be repeated.

Lessons Learned

Healers learned on the job. They had to learn from their mistakes. The first examples of trepanning by the ancient Incas showed that around half died after the operation. But as medical advances such as **anesthesia** and **antibiotics** became more widespread, more people survived. Between AD 1000 and 1400, as many as 91 percent of patients lived.

Today, trepanning is still done, although it's now called craniotomy or craniectomy. It involves specialized equipment, computer assistance, and brain scans. Doctors can remove tumors and blood clots, repair brain injuries, or relieve pressure in the head using modern techniques.

CHAPTER 6
ATTACKING FROM THE INSIDE OUT
GERM THEORY TO VACCINATIONS

When a person is physically injured, it's obvious. But the cause of disease or infection was often a mystery to early doctors.

Some believed a "miasma," or bad air, caused diseases. Others thought diseases just appeared out of nowhere. They did not know that bacteria and viruses were the cause. But that didn't stop doctors from wanting to find an answer.

Smallpox has been one of the most dangerous diseases in human history. Smallpox causes a fever and a rash. The rash leaves small pockmarks on a person's body. The holes develop scabs, which turn into scars.

In ancient India, doctors tried to protect people from this disease in advance. They took scabs off of smallpox victims. Then they had healthy people put the scabs in their noses or mouths.

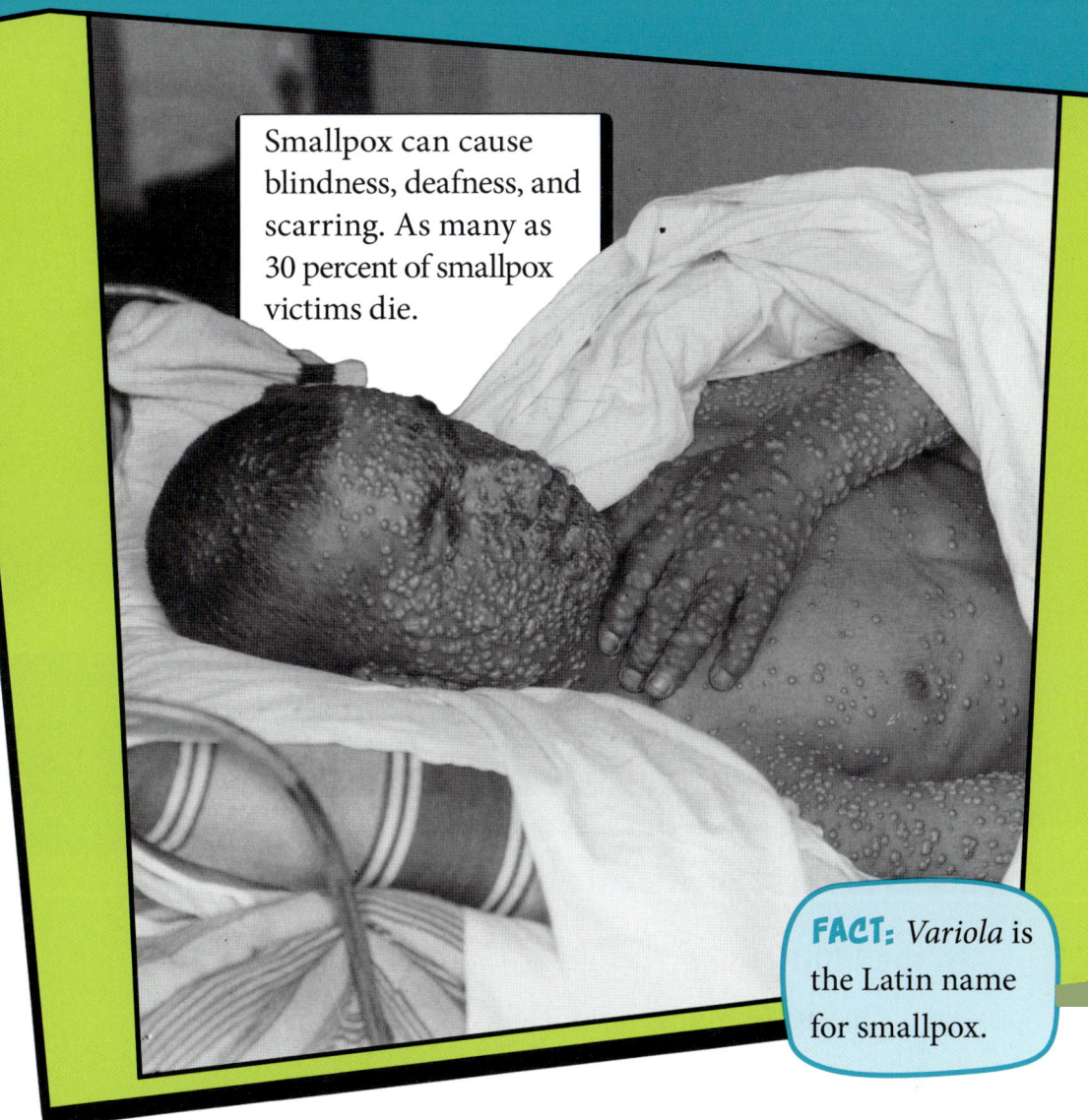

Smallpox can cause blindness, deafness, and scarring. As many as 30 percent of smallpox victims die.

FACT: *Variola* is the Latin name for smallpox.

Purposely infecting a patient with smallpox is called variolation. It was hoped that the healthy people would get a more mild version of smallpox. Then they would be protected from the disease in the future. This worked—sometimes. But some people died. And some people actually spread the full-strength disease to others.

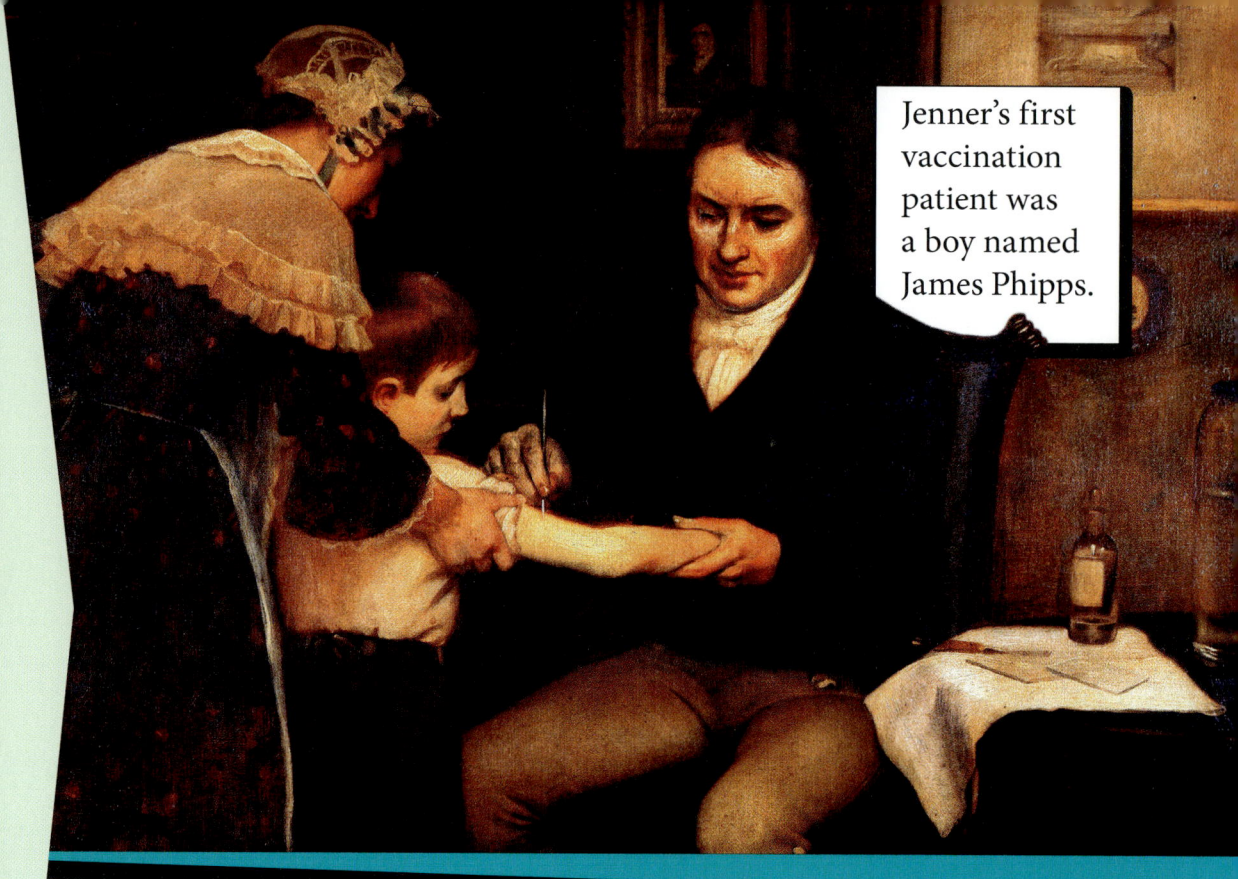

Jenner's first vaccination patient was a boy named James Phipps.

In the 1700s, scientist Edward Jenner had the answer. He knew that women who milked cows didn't get smallpox. But they did experience a similar, but much less dangerous, disease called cowpox. Jenner created the first **vaccine**. He removed fluid from cowpox blisters. Then he injected that fluid into an 8-year-old boy. The boy did not get sick with smallpox.

Jenner continued to test his vaccination with success. The vaccine protected people without making them sick or spreading smallpox to others.

Getting a Closer Look

Ancient physicians knew a sick person could infect another person. But they did not know that germs, viruses, or bacteria cause disease.

Some physicians guessed that "minute creatures" might float through the air and make people sick. Others suggested that "seeds of plague" might stay in a person's body. They were on the right track.

In the late 1600s, scientists developed the microscope and observed **microorganisms**. They started to develop the germ theory of disease. Germ theory states that diseases are caused by germs. Germs, including bacteria and viruses, are too small for people to see with their eyes.

Lessons Learned

The use of vaccines **eradicated** smallpox worldwide by 1977. Other diseases, including chicken pox, influenza, polio, measles, diphtheria, tetanus, yellow fever, and whooping cough have been controlled because of vaccination.

CHAPTER 7
MOLDY MEDICINE
PENICILLIN

Mold isn't usually a good thing. It can cause damage to items and make people sick. But when mold can be used to save lives, it becomes a success story.

In the 1920s, researcher Alexander Fleming was a little careless in his lab. He started an experiment growing bacteria. Then he went on vacation. When he returned home, one of his petri dishes had been bumped, and the lid wasn't on tightly. There was mold growing in his samples.

Fleming thought he would have to throw away that experiment. But when he looked closer, he noticed

FACT: In ancient Egypt, doctors put moldy bread on wounds to help them heal. Modern physicians think the mold on the bread could be similar to penicillin.

Fleming specialized in treating infections and studying bacteria.

that the mold closest to the bacteria made a brown substance. The brown substance killed the bacteria.

Fleming wondered if the mold could be used to kill dangerous bacteria when it was growing in people. The mold was a type called *penicillium*. He called the brown substance penicillin.

It took several years before other doctors took penicillin seriously. The mold was hard to grow. Fleming didn't have the knowledge to produce it in large amounts. The few experiments that had been done weren't always successful. One test on a person looked as though it would work, but the doctors didn't have enough penicillin. In the end, that patient died.

A few dedicated doctors worked on ways to grow penicillin more successfully. By World War II (1939–1945), they were able to

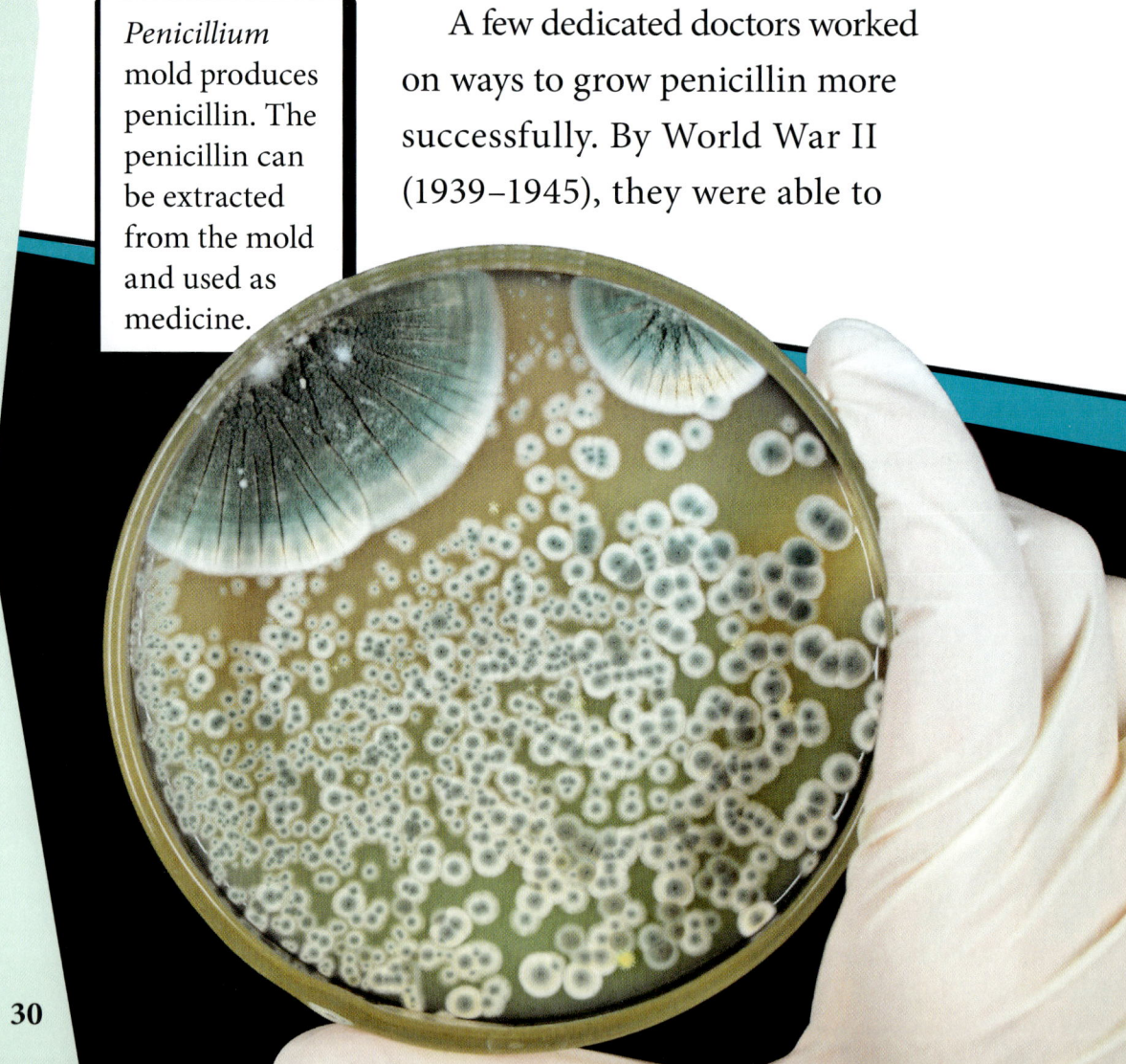

Penicillium mold produces penicillin. The penicillin can be extracted from the mold and used as medicine.

mass-produce the drug. In March 1942, Anne Miller became the first person saved by penicillin. She had been near death, and doctors were out of ideas. They gave her a small dose, and she recovered.

FACT: Alexander Fleming and two men who worked with him were awarded the Nobel Peace Prize in 1945.

Soon penicillin was being used to save lives around the world. During World War I (1914–1918), bacterial pneumonia killed 18 percent of patients. Thanks to penicillin, that number dropped to less than 1 percent by World War II.

Lessons Learned

Fleming said, "I did not invent penicillin. Nature did that. I only discovered it by accident." Sometimes accidents can lead to amazing discoveries! And sometimes it takes the work of many people to make those discoveries successful. Other scientists figured out how to make Fleming's findings available to everyone.

CHAPTER 8

ELECTRIC THERAPY

Early physicians looked for natural treatments and cures for sickness. They used plants and animals to help with illness and injury. One of those animals was the electric eel.

Ancient Romans used a kind of eel called a black torpedo. They would put the eel on the place where a person felt pain. Roman physicians wrote that the spot would go numb. They also used electric eels to try and help people who had mental illness.

In the early 1900s, Albert Abrams claimed electricity could find and cure all kinds of diseases. Abrams invented a device he called the Dynamizer (also sometimes

FACT: Eels haven't disappeared from modern medicine! Doctors have been experimenting with soft, flexible batteries based on the bodies of electric eels. The batteries could help power medical devices, such as pacemakers, in the near future. Pacemakers are placed in a person's chest. They help the heart beat at a healthy rate.

Abrams's inventions were controversial. Some people swore by his methods. Others insisted Abrams was a medical fake.

spelled Dynomizer). The Dynamizer sent an electric current through a person's body. Abrams said it would retune a person's vibrations. He called this treatment radionics.

Abrams claimed he could use radionics to diagnose sick people. He said he could diagnose sick people without seeing them. They could send him their blood and the Dynamizer would tell him what was making them sick.

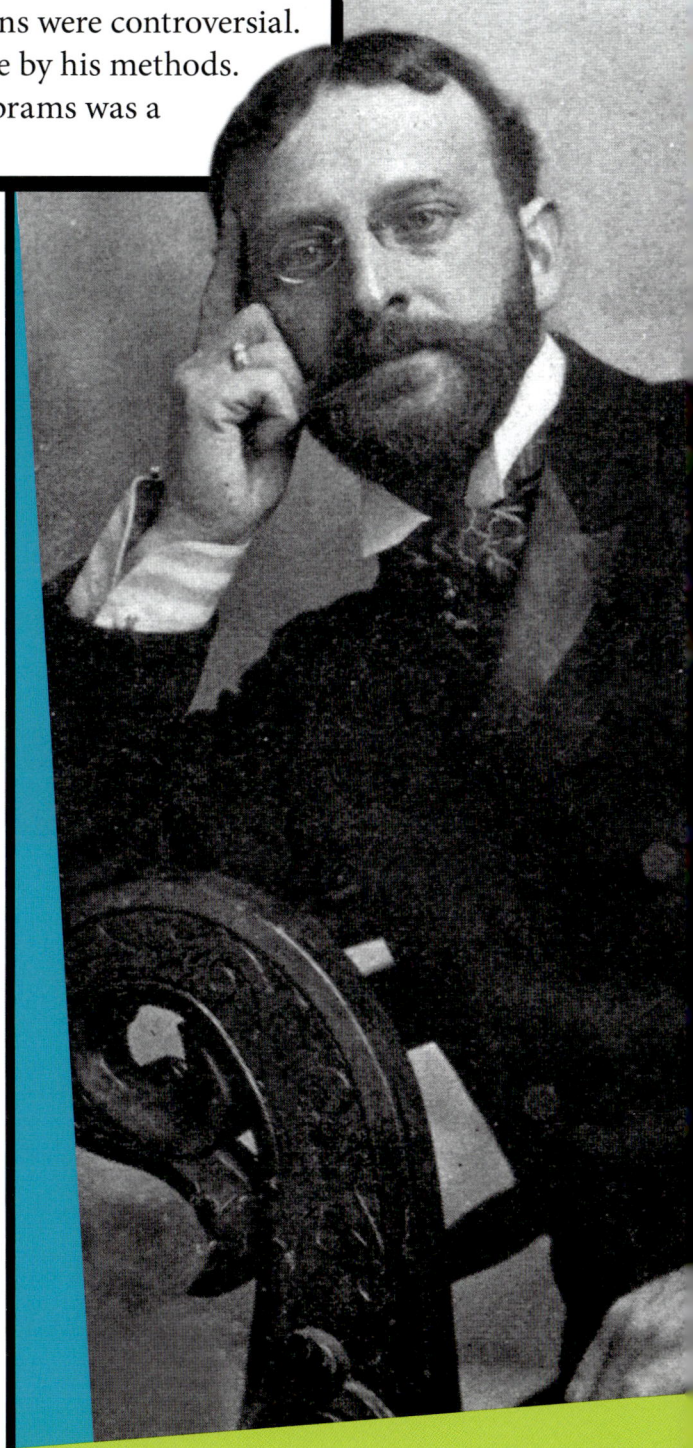

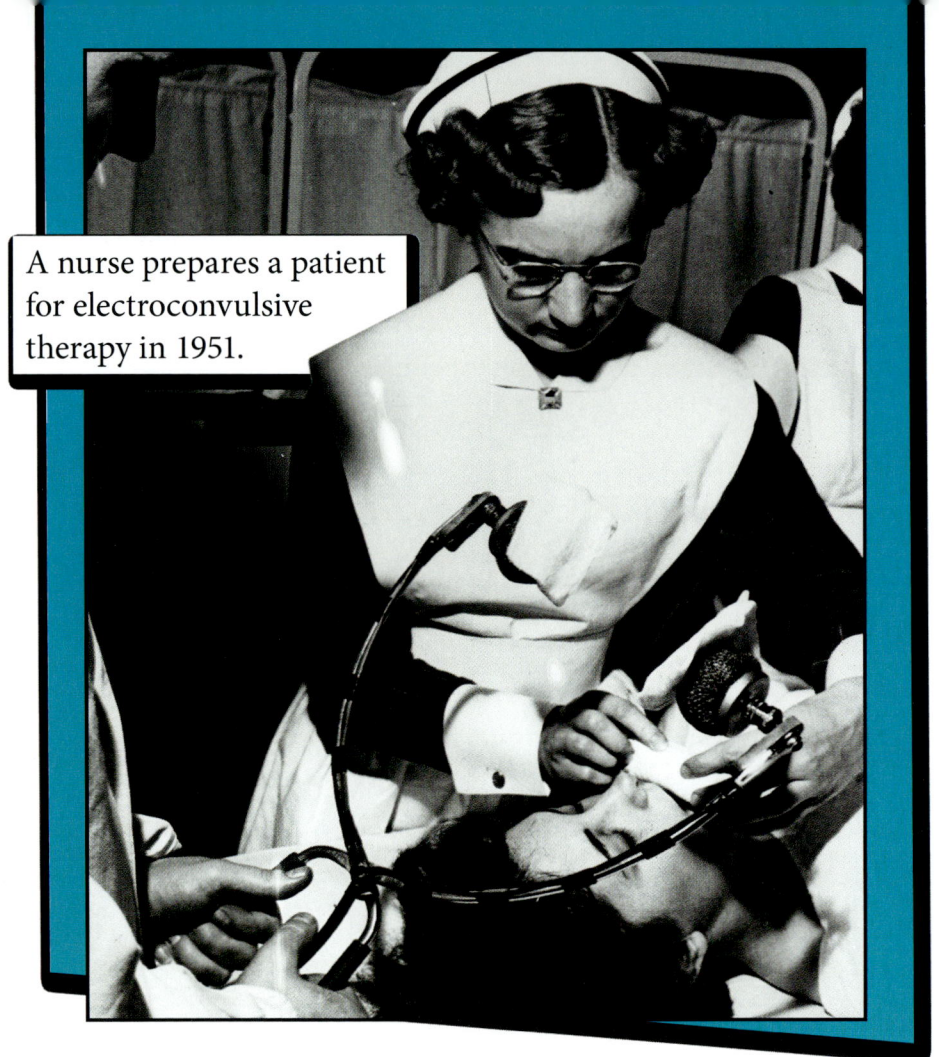

A nurse prepares a patient for electroconvulsive therapy in 1951.

The American Medical Association decided to test Abrams and the Dynamizer. It sent him a blood sample. He said the person had cancer, strep throat, and a sinus infection. But the blood sample was not from a sick person. It was from a guinea pig. Radionics and the Dynamizer were proven to be fakes.

Doctors in the 1930s also used electricity to treat mental illness, but they didn't use eels. They used a treatment called electroconvulsive therapy (ECT). **Electrodes** were attached to a patient's head. Electrical currents were sent through the electrodes and through the person's brain.

ECT helped some people who had depression and **schizophrenia**. The shocks seemed to help reset the way the brain worked. Unfortunately, it was only a temporary fix. After too many treatments, people lost parts of their memory.

Lessons Learned

Scientists and doctors use animals and nature for ideas and inspiration for cures, treatments, and other technological advancements. This is called biomimicry. But no matter how cool their discoveries, there are always limits. It's important to carefully observe how new discoveries affect the people being treated. Sometimes the treatments can do more harm than good.

CHAPTER 9
JUST ZAP IT
RADIATION THERAPY

Radium is a radioactive metal found in the earth. In the early 1900s, physicians discovered that low doses of radium made cancer tumors smaller in some people. Killing cancer cells is a good thing. Doctors thought they had discovered a miracle cure.

Physicians started giving people radium for common problems. They recommended it for joint pain. They prescribed it for dandruff. Feeling tired? Take radium. Teeth not sparkly white? Radium to the rescue! People put radium cream on their face at night and wore radium lipstick during the day.

RADIOACTIVE MATERIALS

Even today, common household materials can contain small—but active—amounts of radium or radioactivity. Different foods can take in radiation through the ground, through the air, and through animals that eat radioactive materials. Bananas, Brazil nuts, and fish are common foods that contain radiation.

- **smoke** detectors
- **watches**
- **fertilizer**
- **ceramic** pottery
- **antique** glass
- **food**

Because it is radioactive, radium glows in the dark. Clockmakers added it to paint and used it to coat clock dials. Women working in the clock factories painted tiny numbers onto clockfaces with this paint. To keep the tips of their paintbrushes sharp, the women licked the brush tips. Every time they licked the paintbrushes, they ingested radium.

Rather than using electric blankets, people were encouraged to use radium compresses instead. The compresses sent out a huge dose of radium, with the promise that there was no danger involved.

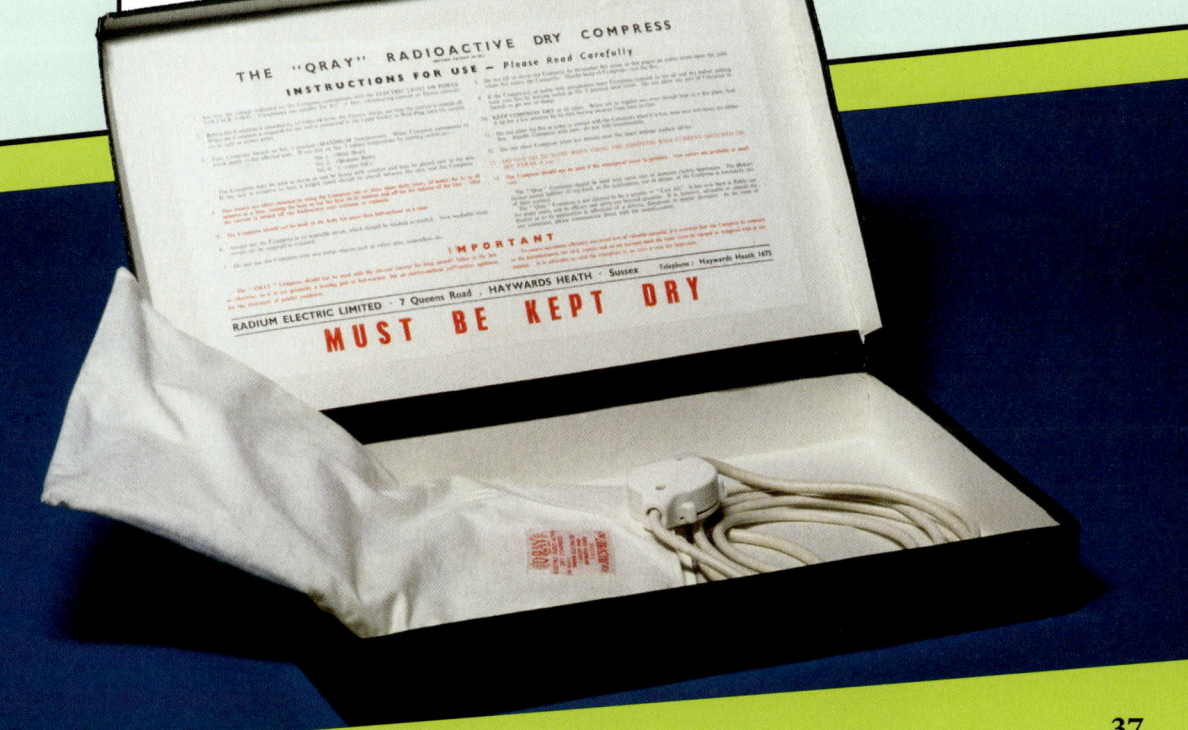

Soon the workers got sick. Their teeth fell out. Their hair fell out. Their bones broke. Some died. Still, people didn't believe radium was the cause.

The radium craze continued. Companies sold radium water. People were encouraged to drink it daily if they didn't feel well. A popular radium water drink was Radithor. The company that made Radithor claimed that it was harmless. But, of course, it was really poison.

FACT: Low doses of radium are used during X-rays.

Radithor was sold between 1925 and 1931. It cost about $1 a bottle, or about $15 today.

The radium trend came to a halt when a rich, popular athlete named Eben Byers became terribly ill. He had been drinking several bottles of Radithor every day for years. He had headaches. His teeth fell out. He lost weight. The bones in his body were disintegrating.

Byers died of radiation poisoning in 1932. By this time, physicians and the public realized radium was toxic. Doctors today know that radium can cause cancer, anemia, vision troubles, and death.

Lessons Learned

Radiation therapy is still useful for treating cancer. But doctors use special equipment and carefully control how much a patient receives. They also limit radium exposure to the part of the body that has cancer.

There are drawbacks, though. Radiation therapy can be expensive. And it can also cause damage to healthy cells. People who undergo radiation therapy often feel tired and have headaches. Blurred vision, hair loss, swelling, shortness of breath, trouble swallowing, and upset stomachs are other side effects.

CHAPTER 10
MY HEAD HURTS!

LOBOTOMIES

Treating mental illness is just as important as treating physical illness. But dealing with the head is always touchy business.

Trepanning was thought to help change a person's behavior. What if removing part of the brain would change his or her thoughts? Portuguese physician Egas Moniz wanted to find out.

Lobotomies are a type of brain surgery. Surgeons drilled a hole in a person's skull or inserted instruments into a person's brain through the eye socket. Then they severed the nerves in the front portion of a human brain. This could be done by drilling holes, injecting alcohol, or poking or scraping the brain with sharp tools.

Moniz created this procedure in 1935. The next year, American psychiatrist Walter Freeman brought the technique to the United States. Both claimed lobotomies would help people who had certain mental illnesses.

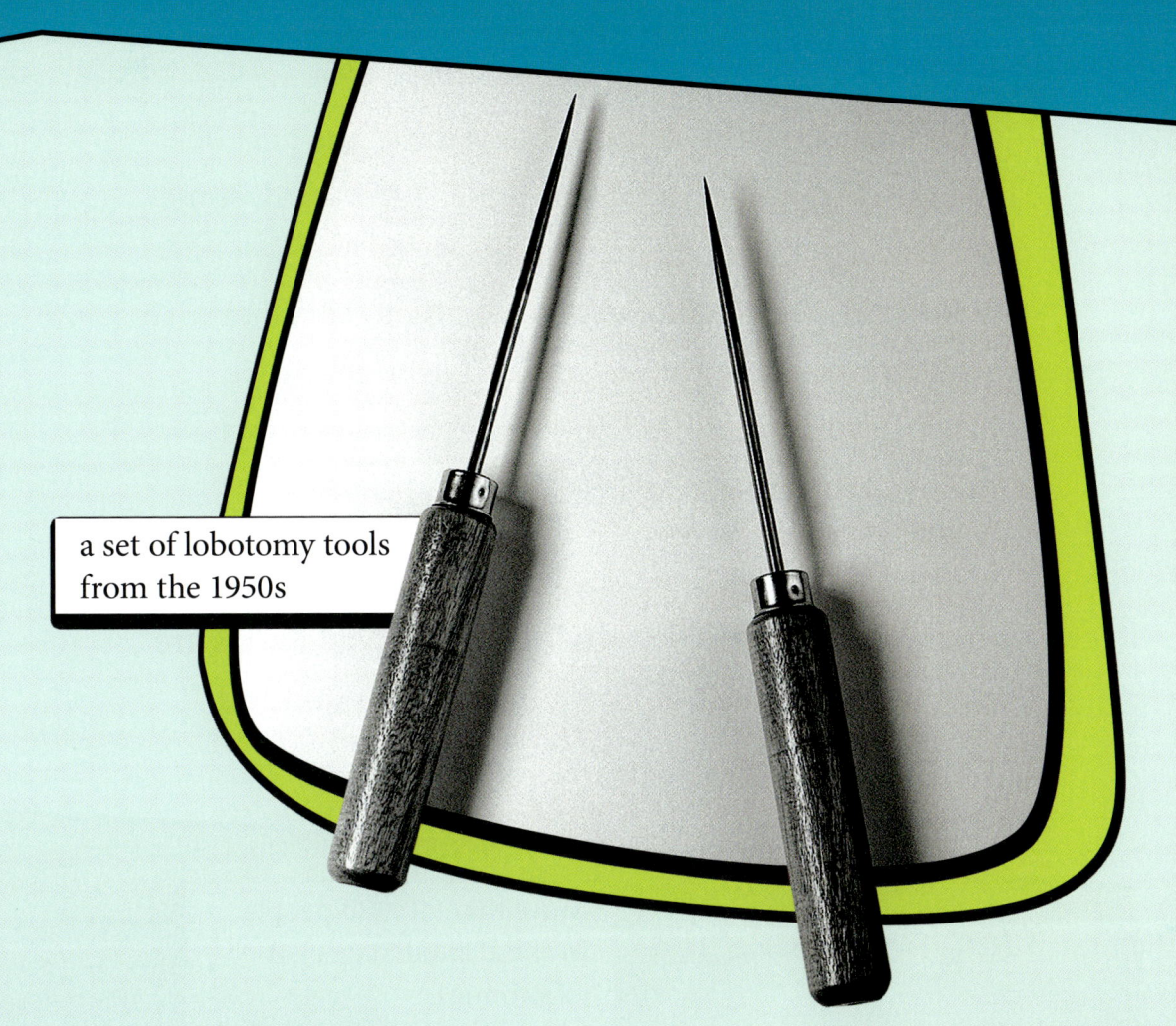

a set of lobotomy tools from the 1950s

Schizophrenia was one of those mental illnesses. People with schizophrenia sometimes act and speak in strange ways. They may have a hard time understanding what is real. Sometimes they hear voices and have difficulty interacting with other people. People with schizophrenia can also be anxious and depressed.

Lobotomies were supposed to remove the part of the brain that caused schizophrenia. Afterward, some patients were less anxious. But others became angry and hostile. They could lose the ability to speak or think clearly. Some people couldn't even take care of themselves anymore. Lobotomies damaged and destroyed important parts of people's brains.

After Moniz received the Nobel Prize in 1949, critics argued that it was undeserved. Nobel Prizes are given for discoveries of "great benefit for mankind."

More than 40,000 people in the United States got lobotomies.

Was something that could rob people of their ability to think for themselves a great benefit?

In 1954, a medicine to treat schizophrenia was released. It was safer and more effective than lobotomies. And it was available to everyone. Lobotomies became unnecessary.

Lessons Learned

Modern-day treatment for schizophrenia includes medication and counseling. Lobotomies are still performed, but rarely. Today, they are known as psychosurgeries. Only patients who have failed to respond to several other forms of treatment can receive it. Doctors study the patient's skull and discuss the best way to enter the brain. Then they use lasers and remove only a tiny amount of brain tissue. Each operation helps them improve their knowledge for next time.

Moniz was on the right track but, like bloodletting, his techniques did more damage than good.

MEDICINE MOVES ALONG

Medical technology is always changing and improving. Researchers and inventors are looking for ways to help. They try to diagnose and treat illnesses and improve the quality of life for people. But many of the new inventions still use old ideas.

Forms of **electricity** have been used for centuries. A new device called the Emma Watch uses electricity to help people who have **tremors**. The Emma Watch sends a small electrical current through a person and minimizes the tremors.

Surgery has been around since prehistoric times. Advances in surgery such as the use of robotic instruments and laser tools make it possible for surgeons to perform complicated surgery.

Ancient Egyptians used the first **artificial limbs**. Thanks to three-dimensional (3-D) printing, researchers can create artificial parts that are as individual as each person who needs them. And they're going beyond arms and legs. A prosthestic voice box can help people speak again after throat surgery. People who have lost their vision can see with the aid of a tiny camera implant.

Physicians experimented with **organ transplants** in the 1800s. The first successful transplants weren't achieved until 1954. Since then they have saved many lives. But to perform transplants, surgeons needed organs, and there are not enough donors to help the people in need. Now researchers are developing ways to create artificial organs using 3-D printing.

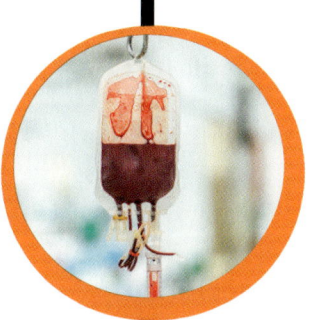

Blood transfusions have been an important part of medicine since the 1800s. Blood transfusions have saved many lives. But blood banks can run out of blood. And it can be difficult to bring blood to many parts of the world. What if scientists could create artificial blood? Right now, researchers have a version of artificial blood that can carry oxygen to human cells.

But the **artificial blood** can't do two important jobs of real blood. It can't form clots, or scabs, when someone is injured. And it can't help carry antibodies from our immune systems around the body. Artificial blood is waiting for a research breakthrough.

GLOSSARY

anesthesia (a-nuhs-THEE-zhuh)—a gas or injection that prevents pain during treatments and operations

antibiotic (an-ti-bye-OT-ik)—a drug that kills bacteria and is used to cure infections and disease

blood transfusion (BLUHD trans-FEW-shuhn)—the act of transferring blood into a person

concentration (kahn-suhn-TRAY-shuhn)—the strength of a solution

diagnose (dy-ig-NOHS)—to find the cause of a problem

electrode (e-LEK-trode)—a point where an electric current can flow into or out of

eradicate (ih-RAD-uh-kayt)—to do away with something completely

membrane (MEM-brayn)—thin, flexible layer of tissue covering surfaces of animal or plant cells

microorganism (mye-kro-OR-guh-ni-zuhm)—a living thing too small to be seen without a microscope

psychiatry (sye-KYE-uh-tree)—the study of treating emotional and mental illness

schizophrenia (skit-suh-FREN-ee-uh)—a mental illness that causes people to see and hear people or things that aren't really there

shock (SHOK)—a medical condition caused by a dangerous drop in blood pressure and flow; people suffering from shock can die

symptom (SIMP-tuhm)—a sign that suggests a person is sick or has a health problem

tremors (TREH-murhs)—involuntary quivers or muscle movement

vaccine (vak-SEEN)—a medicine that prevents a disease

yellow fever (YEL-oh FEE-vur)—an illness that can cause high fever, chills, nausea, and kidney and liver failure; liver failure causes the skin to become yellow, giving the disease its name

READ MORE

Bard, Jonathan. *Oops! It's Penicillin!* New York: Gareth Stevens, 2020.

Krasner, Barbara. *Great Medicine Fails.* Minneapolis: Lerner Publications, 2020.

Rodger, Ellen. *Top Secret Science in Medicine.* New York: Crabtree Publishing, 2019.

INTERNET SITES

KidsHealth.org
https://kidshealth.org

National Institutes of Health
https://www.nih.gov

U.S. National Library of Medicine's Children's Page
https://medlineplus.gov/childrenspage.html

INDEX

Abrams, Albert, 32, 33, 34
Ashoka, 5

bacteria, 24, 27, 28, 29, 31
blood, 4, 12, 13, 14, 15, 16, 17, 18, 19, 33, 34
blood banks, 19
blood donations, 14, 19
bloodletting, 12–15
blood transfusions, 16–19
blood types, 16, 18, 19
Byers, Eben, 39

cancer, 34, 36, 39
cowpox, 26
craniotomy. *See* trepanning

Dynamizer, 32, 33, 34
Dynomizer. *See* Dynamizer

electric therapy, 32–35
electroconvulsive therapy (ECT), 35

Fantus, Bernard, 19
Fleming, Alexander, 28, 29, 30, 31
four humors, 4–7, 13
Freeman, Walter, 40

germ theory, 24–27

Hippocrates, 4, 6

Imhotep, 5
infections, 8, 15, 23, 24, 29

Jenner, Edward, 26

lobotomies, 40, 43
Lower, Richard, 16

Manipal Hospital, 8
medicinal leeches, 14, 15
mental illness, 32, 35, 40, 41
microorganisms, 27
Moniz, Egas, 40, 42, 43

penicillin, 28–31
psychosurgeries.
    See lobotomies

radiation therapy, 36–39
Radithor, 38, 39
reagent strips, 10, 11
Rush, Benjamin, 12, 15

schizophrenia, 35, 41, 42, 43
smallpox, 24, 25, 26

trepanning, 20–23, 40
tumors, 23, 36

urinalysis, 8–11

vaccinations, 24–27
variolation, 25
viruses, 18, 24, 27